W9-BTA-397

Hartland Public Library
P.O. Box 137
Hartland, VT 05048

Boris

CYNTHIA RYLANT

Boris

Hartland Public Library
P.O. Box 137
Hartland, VT 05048

Harcourt, Inc.
Orlando Austin New York
San Diego Toronto London

Copyright © 2005 by Cynthia Rylant

All rights reserved. No part of this publication may be reproduced or
transmitted in any form or by any means, electronic or mechanical,
including photocopy, recording, or any information storage and
retrieval system, without permission in writing from the publisher.

Requests for permission to make copies of any part of the work
should be mailed to the following address: Permissions Department,
Harcourt, Inc., 6277 Sea Harbor Drive, Orlando, Florida 32887-6777.

www.HarcourtBooks.com

Library of Congress Cataloging-in-Publication Data
Rylant, Cynthia.
Boris/Cynthia Rylant.
p.   cm.
1. Cats—Poetry.   I. Title.
PS3568.Y55B67   2005
811'.54—dc22   2004021093
ISBN 0-15-205412-X

Text set in Garamond MT
Designed by Cathy Riggs

First edition
H G F E D C B A

Printed in the United States of America

Boris

1

They were smart
to put a storefront
humane shelter
on the street I walked.
I was new in town.
Everybody else was used
to those cats in cages
in the windows.
They kept on walking,
trained not to glance over,
lest they lie awake
at night thinking about
that long-haired tabby
waiting
waiting
waiting.
But I hadn't been trained.
I tried not to look.
I have never been able

to go to a humane shelter.
But now
they had brought one to me.

I'd buried my last cat
two years before.
I had only dogs now.
Dogs that didn't get into
howling, spitting fights
in the middle of the night.
Dogs that didn't spray
or leave chunks of
frothy hair ball on the
carpet exactly where I
place my feet
in the morning.
I had buried my last cat.
I was a dog person now.
But they'd put a storefront
humane shelter
on the street I walked
every day.
And I was new in town.

I lasted two months.
Then I went inside,
swearing I'd get only one,
and only a girl,
and no more.
Working hard to keep
my heart together.
Cages, cages, eyes.
They can't be too sad.
Cats sleep 80 percent
of the time.
They are all right,
could be worse.
Don't look at that dog
over there.
The one storefront dog
in the cage.
You will break apart.
Not made for shelters.
Ashamed of it.
But not made for shelters.
At first I thought,
I'll choose this one,

this nervous one.
I'll choose this one,
this old battered one.
I'll choose this one,
this bright one.
Cages, cages, eyes.
And then last cage,
last cage,
there you were, Boris.
With your gray sister.
And you stood up
and stretched
and purred
and promised, promised
you would be good if
I took her, too,
because she had
kept you alive
all those days and days and days.
Three months in a cage,
Boris, with your sister,
living in the moment
with only your memories

of leaves and rooftops
and warm brown mice.
I promise, you said,
and I believed you,
and I took home
two cats—one more
than I wanted, and
a boy at that—
but you promised,
and I knew.

2

You spent the first week
hiding
under a down comforter
in the farthest room
at the back of my house
upstairs.
We'd step in softly
to visit you, Boris,
you and your sister.
And, slowly, out you'd come
with a stretch and a yawn.
Not ready for freedom
just yet.
One gets used to a cage,
whether he likes it
or not.
We held you both
on our laps
and spoke your names
as we stroked
your heads.

Near week's end
we had a talk
with the dogs.
We told them
there were two cats
upstairs
they didn't know about
who'd been
listening to all the barking.
We told them to be nice.
Then one of us went in
to sit with you
while the other let
the dogs in, quietly.
You were so fine, Boris.
Not a flinch.
They wagged and sniffed
and pressed closer
and just one little
flick of the ear
was all you gave away
of your alarm.
So fine.
A week later

you and your sister
were downstairs,
fighting for lap space
with the dachshund.
And when you swatted
that stubborn dog's nose one day,
we knew
you were home.

3

There are eagles
where we live, Boris,
and maybe you don't
know this,
but they have
been known to carry off cats.
I even heard
about one eagle
who carried off a dog.
Usually the eagle
overestimates his abilities,
and he drops the dog
or the cat
before he ever gets it back
to the wife and kids
in the nest.
Still, that drop
has got to hurt.
I read about
one cat in a cast

for months.
So listen, Boris,
though I love those eagles,
love them,
you must assume
they are all out to get you,
and you must never,
as I often do,
stand on a beach
beneath them
and say,
"Oh, how beautiful!"
Because one of
them is
at that very moment
measuring you
from head to tail,
pulling out his
calculator and
converting inches into
pounds
and assessing
just what velocity

he'd have to be traveling
to sweep you
off your feet
and have you
over for dinner.
As dinner.
I am hoping, Boris,
that the fish
those eagles
pluck from the water
every morning for breakfast
will never run out,
because if they do,
we are going to
have to feed you nothing but
milk shakes and butter
until we are rolling you
down the beach
every day
and telling those birds
you are just
not
worth the trouble.

4

The rains are starting, Boris,
and we are seeing
much more of you.
There at the door with
your sad, wet cry.
Missing the warm stove
in the garden room
where your sister lies
curled, blissfully
unaware of your absence.
We all need to
come home sometime.
May as well time it
with the winter rain.
For in summer who cares.
We care nothing for
the soft, velvety chair
alongside the reading lamp.
Nothing for the warm
down pillows

on our beds.
The hot showers.
The thick robes.
The cocoa.
In summer we love
less our faithful houses
and pledge our allegiance
to willow trees
and hammocks
and full night moons.
Poor houses.
Waiting patiently
till we finally
appreciate the
roofs that don't leak,
the doors that don't squeak,
and the furnace
that works.
We are like you, Boris.
We are outside cats
and proud of it
until the first big drop
of rain hits our noses

and we run for the door,
leaving our free spirits
behind us,
crawling into someone's lap.

5

They were guessing at the shelter
when they said you
might be four, Boris.
You could have been
seven or eight.
Somebody who has, as they say,
been around the block.
Were you hoping they'd
subtract a few years,
filling out that cat form?
Because you know
how the world is.
You're just cruising along,
minding your own business,
not paying much attention
to the number of Christmases
rolling by.
Then one day no one
thinks you're cute anymore.
Is cuteness a must

in the cat world, Boris?
It is in mine.
And beyond a certain age,
cuteness is an impossibility.
Nothing left but character,
and that won't get you a
good table at a restaurant
or a warning
instead of a speeding ticket.
I know the shelter
was the pits, Boris.
I don't mean to minimize it.
But I can think of a lot
of years
I wish I'd been given a fresh start.
Past wiped out.
New identity.
A few years shaved off.
But they don't allow it
here in my world.
Here in my world
the forms go on forever
and they hold you

like a fly in amber.
Forever in that petri dish,
forever exactly who
your parents and your schools
and your government numbers
say you are.
It is impossible to go back
and start over.
Nearly impossible to disappear.
Were you really four, Boris,
when I found you?
No matter.
Be who you are.

6

I heard them last night,
Boris,
that pack of dogs that occasionally
runs through the neighborhood.
With my window open,
I heard them barking
and grunting
and sniffing
and panting
just outside,
on the trail of who knows what,
but glad it wasn't you,
Boris,
glad it wasn't you.
How did you know
to stay in?
Whenever they've
been through here,
every three months or so,
you've been tucked in

the house somewhere,
downstairs
curled with your sister,
ears sharp and twitching
as you listen to
those clumsy, dangerous
dogs outside.
How did you know
to stay in?
Was there rumor
of a rumble
buzzing the street yesterday?
Did someone—
say, that calico
four doors down—
tell you, *Stay in, man.*
Something is going down.
And though you
are willing to die in
an eagle's talons
or a coyote's jaw
or even by car,
you are not going

to let a pack of
house dogs with
their decorated collars and
jingling tags,
bellies full of
Kibbles 'n Bits,
take you down.
Cowards.
Following the pack.
You are more than that,
Boris, and you know it.

Discreetly you slip inside
and listen, silent,
to their hysteria.

7

They told me at
the shelter, Boris,
that your name before
was Hunter.
And I thought, *Yes,
a nice upper-middle-class,
designer-label sort of
name.*
Not a bad name at all,
though not one I'd choose.
So I named you Boris instead,
and you knew who you were
within a day.
You knew that you
were Boris.
Smart kitty.
But even though you
answered quite nicely,
you let me understand,

over time,
that you had, in fact, been
Hunter and that,
like one of those mysterious men
on the soaps
with the hidden past
that won't go away,
you were still
that guy.
Because it didn't take
long for the
half-dead mice to start
swooning all over
the patio,
the beautiful, delicate
birds to seemingly
drop dead on my steps,
the goldfish to disappear
from my neighbor's pond,
and the one big rabbit to show up.
The dead one.
Hunter.

I'd thought it was
old New England Hunter,
prep-school Hunter,
that particular shade of green Hunter.
But it was *hunter* Hunter.
Didn't ring a bell
until maybe the fifteenth
mouse.
Well, someone tried to warn me, Boris.
Whoever named you first.
Remove all bird feeders was
the message.
But I am slow and naive, Boris.
You knew that,
didn't you,
coming right away
when I first called your name.
So, Boris it is, you must have thought,
tossing your old name tag off the side of a bridge.
But, like those nervous, troubled characters
in nineteenth-century literature,
every now and then

you are that *other* guy.
That one who lives in the cellar.
Hunter.

8

We heard a new cat
was moving in next door
and we thought,
Oh no.
That cat is doomed.
Boris has been sitting
on the next-door deck
for two years, we said.
He's tagged it
again and again
with his
instantly portable
cat spray.
Everybody listen
loud and clear:
That is *Boris's turf.*
The cat is doomed.
Desperate, we took you to the vet
for some plastic claws.
Nice little fake plastic claws

that stick on over
your lethal ones.
We could not
take the chance
that some night
the new neighbors
who were foolish enough
to move next door
with a *cat*
(what were they thinking?)
would show up on our steps
with a bag full of
shredded fur and teeth
and eyes
that used to be
somebody named Fluffy.
What else could we do?
But you managed, didn't you,
Boris,
to still climb trees
with your sharp back claws
while we waited for
the new cat to move in.

Then finally, one day,
he arrived.
Harvey.
A six-month-old
piece of gray dust ball
named Harvey.
On *your* deck, Boris.
Stupid kid.
We waited to see if
you would tear him
to bits with your teeth.
Annihilate him
with a million plastic jabs.
Drop him
like a mouse at our door
and look for praise.
Harvey, we feared,
was not long for this world.
We were wrong.
Boris, you sly cat,
you poser,
you swaggering
bowl of jelly.

You adopted him.
You adopted Harvey,
and mornings we'd look out
and there you'd be,
teaching Harvey to jump,
teaching Harvey to pounce,
playing chase through
the tall reedy grass.
That deck, that infamous deck,
became where you two
sunned yourselves
after the fun and games,
and we could not believe it.
You liked him, that kid.
Reminded you of yourself
when you were just a
young upstart
looking for a role model.
And maybe you'd heard
Harvey's sad story.
About being out on the streets
of Nashville,
begging.

He got to you, didn't he, Boris?
So when the plastic claws
dropped off after
three months,
we didn't replace them.
By that time you were
going into Harvey's house
for supper
and sleeping with Harvey
at the foot of their bed
and generally just
being a big pussy.
As Harvey grew,
he looked just like you, Boris,
sleek and gray
and green-eyed.
No one could have told you apart
if not for Harvey's bell.
And when he moved away, Boris,
you left a big bag of
treats on Harvey's doorstep
and a note that read
"You're a good kid,"

and you wished him luck,
one guy to another,
sure he'd be okay:
You taught him
everything he knows.

9

You disappeared
for ten days, Boris.
And for nine of them
I imagined
what it must have
been like for you,
being cornered by a coyote.
The wild fear.
The first broken bone.
The small yellow cat collar
with "BORIS 962-7899"
in Sharpie,
left behind in the leaves.
I hated for you
to have to go that way, Boris.
Though I'd seen what you'd
done to mice
and I knew it was justice.
Still, maybe there was a small part of me
relieved

that I didn't have to have
a hand in your death.
Because I know what it is
to take a dying pet
on its final journey,
how each passing moment
counts so terribly,
and how that crescendo
toward death
builds and builds
until one can hardly bear
another second of impending doom
and utter end.
I know what it is,
that awful sudden instant
when the breathing stops
and someone is gone forever.
And one wants to die, too, then,
so as not to
feel anymore.
I don't want
to live that again.
I want everyone I love

to die in sleep,
and preferably
after I've left the planet myself.
So, Boris, as I looked
for your remains
beneath shrubs
and in ditches
when the dogs and I
were out for our walks,
I knew that if I found you dead,
at least you spared me
being part of the thing.
You were good enough
to do that for me.
But on the tenth day, Boris,
you came home.
There you were, sitting at the patio door,
waiting for me to get out of bed.
After ten days missing,
you came home.
Skinny.
Hungry.
A bloody front paw.

And as I carried you inside,
I knew
this had been no
mere adventure.
Boris, you had won
a *battle*.
You had won a battle
in the thick forest where we live,
and there was no witness
to your bravery.
But I know.
I know, Boris,
that somewhere
a coyote wanders,
one eye dangling from its socket,
and tufts of
gray fur in his jaw.
You are keeping closer to home now, Boris,
and that's good.
Don't feel sheepish.
Don't think we care
that the forest

no longer calls to you.
Because you are a fine boy, Boris.
A cat of cats.
You survived.

10

I thought that maybe,
after the last dog
passes away,
I'll get a condominium.
(Which I'll prefer to
call an apartment,
though technically
it would be a condo,
even if I cringe
at the word.)
I didn't want to be
that girl,
the one who
lives in a condo.
I'm the person
who baked bread
in college,
wore long skirts
and boots
and didn't own

an iron (still don't)
or nylons (ditto).
I wanted to
be a cool hippie
but I'm not really.
I am too misanthropic
to live in a commune,
and the phrase
"Peace and love"
grates on my nerves.
Still, I have always
known for sure
I am not a condo girl.
Aren't condos for people
who drive Buicks
and collect glass figurines?
Those people who think
Vegas is a destination
and *Friends* is funny?
But I am tired.
Tired of weatherproofing
and leaf blowing
and WD-40.

Tired of owning a house.
Wasn't I supposed to live
in one of those
beautiful brownstones I saw
in *101 Dalmatians* when
I was six?
That's who I wanted to be.
That pretty woman,
that urban chick
with the brownstone
and the cool dog.
Well, where I live
brownstone means
condo,
and that brings me
to you, Boris.
Already I can hear you
saying, *No way.*
No way are you going to
live with me on the
fifth floor with
just a pathetic little
balcony to sit on

day after day
and not a clue
about how to operate
that elevator out
in the hall.
I want to be a
cool, urban chick,
Boris,
and you want a lawn.

You win.

11

It's clear by now, Boris,
that we shouldn't have
bought that kitty video.
Look at what it's made you:
an ottoman potato.
We pulled the ottoman up
as close to the screen
as we could,
and now that it's cold outside
and you've never
been much of a reader,
all you do
is sit in front of that video
and bat at the birds
on TV.
What's worse—
besides our slight
dismay that we
know you're being tricked
and you don't—

what's worse
is that we're missing
all our favorite shows.
It's the usual family crisis:
one TV and everyone
wants to watch it.
We tried to get you interested
in our shows, Boris,
but you just
don't get the jokes.
And nobody even moves
on that one game show.
You like
TV that moves.
That's why you love
your kitty video.
Birds fly in,
birds fly out.
Just like outside.
Except now
we all sit and watch you
watch the birds.
What would the pioneers think

if they could see us?
They knew what to do
with their evenings.
Dip candles,
make socks,
sharpen their
thingamajigs.
This is why people
are so pessimistic
about the world today.
Because we've given up
making socks
to watch cats
sit in front of TVs.
Of course,
how many yuks
did those pioneers get,
sewing and dipping?
Not many,
I'd say.
Probably none.
But when we watch you
rise up on your hind legs, Boris,

and take a swing
at that television,
well,
all we do is laugh.
We laugh *every time*.
You still don't get the joke, Boris,
but it doesn't matter
because you're having fun
and we're having fun.
And years and years
from now
we are going to say,
"Remember when
Boris watched TV?"
and we're going to
have a really good laugh
which, I repeat,
is more than the
pioneers ever had
sewing their
warm and serious socks.

12

I know how you love her, Boris,
your sister,
and I,
an only child,
envy you.
Animals are lucky.
They are almost always
part of a litter.
And wasn't it wonderful,
when you were a baby, Boris,
to sleep in a pile
of brothers and sisters,
all that warm breathing,
and the knowing
you were not alone?
You should see how
we humans do it.
We have one baby
at a time, mostly,
and as soon as it is born

we put it in a box
all by itself
and though we put
warm booties on its feet
and a little hat on its head
and wrap it up
snug in a blanket,
that baby is far from snug.
That baby is
going to scream
for *hours*
and everyone is
going to think
it's gas,
but, really, Boris,
it's because God forgot to
make people
in litters.
How many baby kittens
do you see
screaming for hours?
None.
Who would,

curled up in
a big pile of fur
and feeling somebody
lick your ears
now and then.
Why is it God
forgot to give
humans company?
Even if a human
is lucky enough
to have a brother
or a sister,
it takes nearly a year
of waiting
and even then
it's a disappointment
because all they
do is scream.

I have lived
a good while, Boris,
and I have never
gotten used to

being alone.
But you, Boris,
you have always
had your sister
and this is why
you don't go looking
for new friends,
as I do,
or haunt the coffee shops,
as I have,
or worry that
no one likes you.
You have always
had
someone
to come home to.

13

Boris likes to play spinnies.
That's when we put you down
on the hardwood floor,
all stretched out,
and we give you a twirl.
Around you go.
Spinnies!
We get you going like
a merry-go-round,
and you lose every ounce
of feline dignity
as you whip around
at our whim,
and we are delighted
by your silliness.
But when you get tired
of the game
and try to walk away
and we say,
"One more time, Boris,"

that's when we
see the tiger in your eyes.
That's when the big cat
on that little circus stool
just an inch from eating
his trainer if there's one more flaming
hoop to jump through
shows up in your eyes, Boris.
And you take that spinnie
in stride,
but we all know,
we all know,
you are humoring us
and we are on very thin ice
indeed
and suddenly
it is we who look so silly,
big dumb humans
giggling at spinnies
when we should be
building rocket ships
and making art
instead of giving Boris a go

one more time.
It must be then
such a thin thread
between love and hate
for you, Boris.
And only because you
are better than we are
and more noble
and patient
and with a real ability
to weigh things in the balance
that you forgive us
and take one last ride
before you get up and walk away
like it was no big deal,
just going with the flow,
no problem.
Saving face, Boris, as you
leave us in that
big empty space on
the floor
with our
dull imaginations

and embarrassing
lack of control.

But can we do spinnies
tomorrow?

14

Boris, you weren't supposed to
beat up an old cat.
Yes, he was new to the neighborhood.
Yes, he was on *your* walking path.
But, Boris, he was
seventeen years old
for godsakes.
Arched and hobbling like
a bent-up coat hanger.
And didn't you admire him,
just a little,
the way he insisted on
following his owner to
the end of the path,
though it must have
seemed a day's journey to him,
that path you streaked across
in seconds?
And, Boris, even worse,
you hid in the tall grass

and pounced.
Didn't even face him
like a man.
There is a word for
you today, Boris,
and it is *thug*.
But how can we not
love you anyway.
And not sympathize,
at least a little,
with your desire to
knock that decrepit
old cat to kingdom come,
because in him
there is your future,
and mine.
There we are, Boris,
in a blink of time,
and don't you hate
being reminded of it?
I do.
Checking the mirror
every day

to see how nearer
I've come to that.
To that pathetic old cat
trying to stay on the path
until it ends
where the bright water is,
and the seabirds,
and the sun.
Not giving all that up just yet.
Even when some young
whippersnapper
says it's time.

15

The accountant's wife
came and knocked
on my door one night
and told me you'd
come in through her
pet flap
and sprayed
her couch, Boris.
Plus scratched her cat.
Plus she came home
one day and found you
sleeping upstairs
in the middle of her bed.
She is one of those
taut little women
who wears jogging clothes.
I knew those girls in college,
those girls you'd avoid
in the dorm bathroom
because you knew

they were going to sure see to it
that you didn't have
too much fun, missy,
you and your happy friends.
Girls like that
become accountant's wives
in jogging clothes
who tell people
to get rid of their cats
for acting like cats
and who think
if they cut holes
in the walls of their houses
they have a right to complain
if someone *uninvited* steps in.
And sprays and scratches
then takes a nap.
At first I said sorry, sorry.
I'm so sorry.
I'll find him a new home.
Then I came to my senses.
Accountant's wife: Screw you.
I know your kind.

I'm keeping my cat,
so just plug up your hole.
And while you're at it,
cover that
stupid pet flap.

16

Where do you go at night, Boris?
Where do you go that I can't,
being a girl who knows better
than to
roam alleyways
in the dark,
the one lesson from my
adolescence that stuck.
But let me tell you a
secret, Boris.
I used to know the
night, too.
When I was ten and
the world wasn't
what it is,
I used to creep
out over the dark wet grass
to the shed out back
whose roof I could climb on
and, catlike,

sit and watch and listen.
It is exquisite
to be alone in the dark,
a feeling of danger
at the edges,
but there's your
house right there,
there's the door,
don't worry.
Is this what it is for you, Boris,
sitting on the neighbor's roof
in the black night
and seeing my window there?
Can you hear my breathing,
the dogs' deep sighs,
your sister's purr
carrying over the
rippling night air?
And do you think, Boris,
how terribly beautiful
it all is,
this world that
lives in a frenzy all day,

then drops
limp
like a new baby
into the deep sleep of night?
When I was ten
and on a roof,
I may have thought
such things.
In the silent black of night,
only deep reassurances
fill the mind,
and it is a safe world
for children and cats,
and God is not so lost.

17

Dogs are all the same
at the animal hospital.
You've seen them, Boris.
Pacing and complaining
and peeing on the floor.
And the cats,
with their heads tucked
inside their owners' bellies,
they aren't much better.
How is it then, Boris,
that you are so
magnanimous
when you arrive?
Sitting quietly in your
kitty bag,
taking stock of
all the wimps
around you,
pausing now and then
to wash your pretty feet.

And when I carry you
into the examining room
it is *you* who does
the examining.
Freed from your bag,
you move from table to
chair to table,
inspecting all the instruments
and spray bottles
and that big jar of dog treats
behind the soap.
Taking your time.
And when the doctor
walks in,
you are stretched out
on that stainless-steel counter,
humming a tune
and wondering if anybody
is up for a game of Scrabble.
Outside in the waiting room,
the waiting and pacing
and crying and moaning
goes on,

but in here, Boris,
everything's cool,
we are so very cool,
and the man you now
refer to as Doc is
admiring your
thick gray coat and your
sharp white teeth,
and your purr is making the
room tremble.
A hospital takes
the measure of a man,
Boris, and you are the
manliest man of a cat
any of us has ever seen.
Tossing a dozen dog biscuits
into your kitty bag,
you say *sayonara*
when the exam is done,
and the doctor retreats quietly
into his office
to pop a couple
testosterone pills,

while out in the waiting room
the place falls into a hush
as you pass by,
already curled up
with the latest copy of *Cat Fancy*
in one paw
and a martini
in the other.

18

I know I probably shouldn't
mention the other male cats
who came before you, Boris.
It doesn't take a girl
long
to find out
how touchy men are
about old boyfriends.
No matter *how* much
you're dying to tell
the guy you're with
about the time
your old boyfriend
made you drive
a stick shift in the
middle of the night
on the way to Myrtle Beach
even though you'd
only driven automatics
and he went to sleep

and left you there on
the freeway trying to
downshift from fourth
to third
so you could catch
that exit ramp
coming up,
and the thrill of that,
that you managed it
with *no* lessons,
or that other boy
you jumped out of the plane
to impress
and floated down at 5,000 feet
only to realize
a couple days later
he was gay
and you nearly
splattered yourself
all over Dayton, Ohio, for him,
even though it's a great story,
DON'T TELL IT.
So maybe, Boris,

I shouldn't tell you
about the others.
About Audience and Beckett
and Louie and Tobias
and Edward, dear Edward,
whom I found dead
by the side of the road,
after coming home from
a funny movie,
and the awfulness
that I'd been
having a good laugh
at the moment of impact
when that car
slammed into him
and, God, I hope
killed him instantly.
Everyone loved Edward.
Can I tell you that, Boris?
That when a couple
came to buy my house
they wanted Edward with it
and they weren't kidding.

He was a sweetheart,
loved to ride on my shoulders.
He'd been abandoned like you, Boris.
You two would have had
a lot to talk about.
Yes, there have been others.
But there never was
nor ever shall be
another Boris,
you can believe me
when I say it,
and I tell you we are
here now together
to make our mark,
you and I,
in this brief moment
before we lie down
to an eternal sleep
among the roses.
There have been other cats, Boris,
but of those who disappeared and are
maybe still alive,
one of them is probably

telling some other human
that she's not the first
he's loved.
No, there was that other one,
years ago,
with the small blond boy
and all the goldfish
and that constant
Beatles music.
Boris, if you live someday
with another person,
please be kind
when you speak of me,
and explain that, yes, I
was maybe now and then
too alone,
but that I
made you happy,
and that you
made me happy, too.

19

Last December I moved
one state south,
and that night, Boris,
you and your sister
were put in kitty-crates
and were driven
six long hours
squeezed in the
back of the van
with the dogs,
the Labrador
panting like a bellows,
the corgi
throwing up on her bed,
the dachshund
whining and wanting some
immediate answers *now.*
What were you thinking, Boris?
Were you remembering
how it was at the shelter,

how they hauled
you and your sister in crates
from the main building
to the little storefront building
every morning,
and put you in the window
for everyone to see,
then hauled you back
again at night?
Did you learn to hate
a crate?
Did you learn
that vans suck?
What must you
have been thinking, then,
when you were
put in the back of my van,
in a crate,
and driven six long hours south.
Did you think
you were going back, Boris?
Back to that big main building?
And did you take one

last look
at the lattice fence
you loved to stroll on,
and the poplar tree
you loved to climb,
and the house where
the triplets gave you shrimp?
Did you work
on your attitude,
those six long hours
in the van,
and tell yourself
you could live in a cage again
if that's the way it is?
Life isn't perfect.
And were you ready, Boris,
to say good-bye to me
up until the very moment
the van stopped
and you were lifted out
and carried into
a house
that had the same old furniture

you'd been clawing up for three years,
and a warm fire
in a large stove,
and, yes,
even your favorite
brand of kitty litter.
If your life passed
before your eyes, Boris,
between the old house
and the new one,
then we are
made of the same stuff.
Because I, too, have mourned
the passing of fences
and yards
and small children
as I drove away
from an old life
on my way somewhere else
where I hoped maybe I'd find
something that was missing.
I have never managed this
without tears.

But isn't it so, Boris,
that every new place
has such beautiful trees
and a blue sky
in the morning.
Isn't it so,
that every new place
is worth trying.
Here, we walk among
the cedars, Boris,
hope in our hearts,
three happy dogs
in tow.